WHERE CRANES ARE FOUND

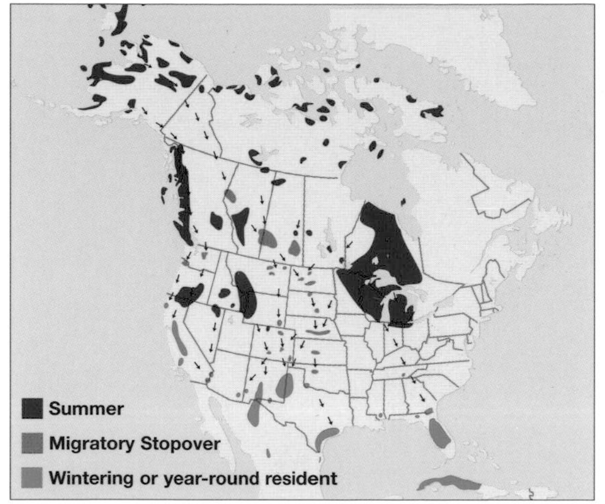

Most populations of Sandhill cranes nest in the north during the summer and migrate to the south for the winter as indicated by arrows.

Excellent locations to view cranes include:

- **Iain Nicolson Audubon Center at Rowe Sanctuary** near Kearney and the **Crane Trust Nature and Visitor Center** near Grand Island, Nebraska (center of the spectacular mid-continent spring staging in the Platte River Valley);
- **Columbia National Wildlife Refuge (NWR)** near Othello, Washington (spring staging);
- **Ridgefield NWR and Sauvie Island Wildlife Area** along the Columbia River near Portland, Oregon (fall and spring staging);
- **Alamosa and Monte Vista NWRs** in the San Luis Valley, Colorado (spring and fall staging);
- **Creamer's Field Migratory Waterfowl Refuge** in Fairbanks, Alaska, and near Homer, Alaska (April - September);
- **Crex Meadows Wildlife Area** near Grantsburg, WI (fall staging);
- **Jasper-Pulaski Fish & Wildlife Area**, in Indiana (fall staging);
- **Hiwassee Refuge** near Birchwood, Tennessee, and Barren River Lake in south-central Kentucky (fall and spring staging);
- **Merced, Stone Lake & Sacramento NWRs** and **Cosumnes River Preserve** near Lodi, California (winter);
- Saline ponds in playas south of Willcox, Arizona (winter);
- **Bosque del Apache, Bitter Lake and Grulla NWRs** in New Mexico (winter);
- **Muleshoe and Laguna Atascosa NWRs** in Texas (winter).

In Florida, Mississippi and Cuba, resident nonmigratory crane populations live within parks, golf courses, and housing subdivisions where they can be easily approached throughout the year.

We used photographs of Sandhill cranes in Alaska to illustrate displays for this guide. Other crane populations may have different dialects in their body language. For more information and links to scientific literature on crane behaviors, go to the website: **www.AlaskaSandhillCrane.com**

Waterford Press publishes reference guides that introduce readers to nature observation, outdoor recreation and survival skills. Product information is featured on the website: **www.waterfordpress.com**

By Christy Yuncker Happ and George M. Happ with helpful suggestions from George Archibald. Photographic images provided by Christy Yuncker Happ. Map adapted from Paul Johnsgard by Raymond Leung. Text & illustrations © 2011, 2023 by Waterford Press and Christy Yuncker Happ.

 To order or for information on custom published products please call 800-434-2555 or email orderdesk@waterfordpress.com. For permissions or to share comments email editor@waterfordpress.com. 2301501

$7.95 U.S.
$9.95 CAN
ISBN 978-1-58355-690-0
50795
9 781583 556900
UPC 8 84682 00879 6
10 9 8 7 6 5 4 3 2
Made in the USA

SANDHILL CRANE DISPLAY DICTIONARY – What Cranes Say with Their Body Language   Yuncker/Happ

A POCKET NATURALIST® GUIDE

SANDHILL CRANE DISPLAY DICTIONARY

What Cranes Say with Their Body Language

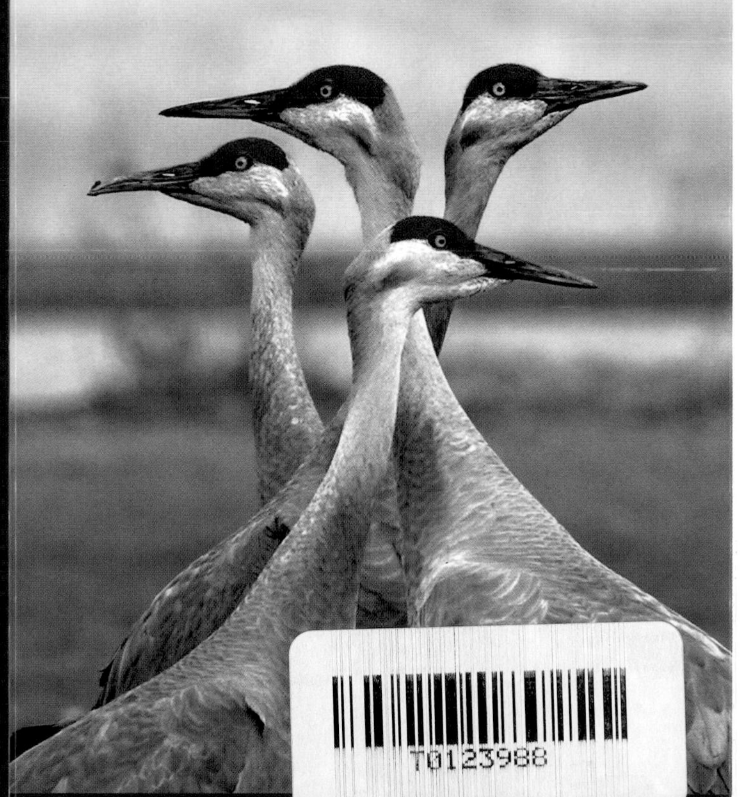

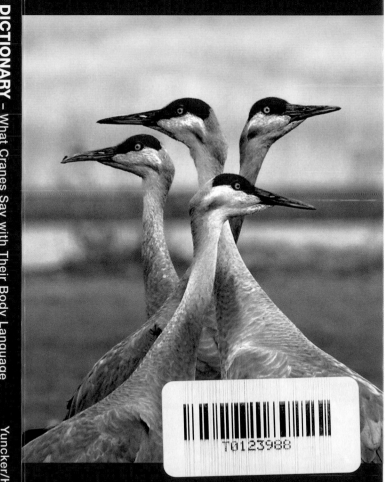

www.AlaskaSandhillCrane.com

SOCIAL BODY LANGUAGE

Sandhill cranes are one of the oldest known bird species on Earth with fossils dating back two million years. These 4-foot (1.2 m) tall, vociferous, gray-brown birds with long, black legs have 6-foot (1.8 m) wingspans and expressive red crowns. Cranes mate for life and migrate in extended families, although some populations along the Gulf Coast and Cuba do not migrate. Central flyway cranes (greater, lesser, and Canadian subspecies) overwinter in gregarious flocks in Texas, New Mexico, Arizona and northern Mexico. Every spring, they fly thousands of miles, showing their cinnamon-colored juveniles the route. The Platte River in Nebraska remains one of the longer spectacular stopovers, where 500,000 cranes replenish their dwindling energy reserves. In long undulating skeins, high in the sky, sounding like the roar of a crowd, the cranes continue north to nest across the northern US, Canada, Alaska and even eastern Siberia.

Crane body language shows arousal, recruits others to dance, preserves the nest territory, announces intent, establishes dominance, and bonds male and female pairs.

What should you watch in order to translate the body language?

- **Crown/reddish forehead skin** – Large or small?
- **Feathers** – Fluffed or sleeked? Is the bustle up or down?
- **Posture** – Standing erect? Leaning forward? Jumping? Pecking toward the ground? Crouched down?
- **Wing position** – Folded back? Held out? Spread wide? Held low?
- **Neck posture** – Coiled back? Held out straight? Held high or low?
- **Movement** – Walking quickly? Pacing carefully? Running? Wing flapping? Bill jabbing?
- **Bill** – Pointing forward? Up? Down? Pecking the ground?
- **Direction of gaze** – What is the target of the display? Remember that each eye looks to the side with a field of vision that is nearly 180°.

Intend-to-fly

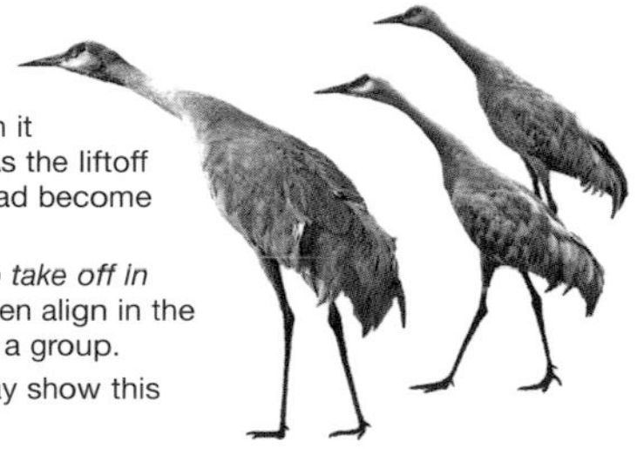

Display: Crane points in the direction it intends to fly and emits a soft purr. As the liftoff becomes imminent, the neck and head become more horizontal.

Function: *"Get ready. We're going to take off in this direction."* Associated cranes often align in the same posture and then all take off in a group.

As young cranes learn to fly, they may show this display before taking off.

Unison call

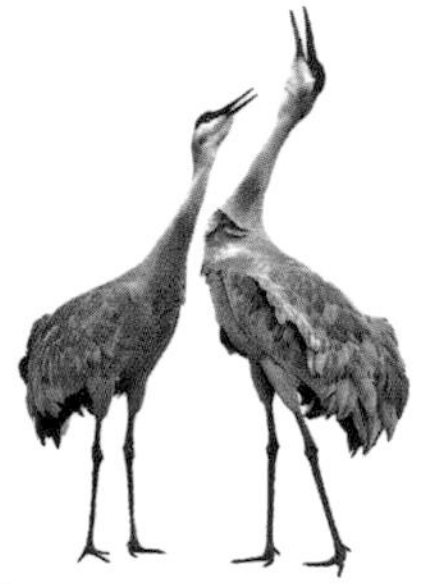

Display: Male and female stand side-by-side with necks upright. The male (right in photo) flips his head upward as he calls, and the female lifts her head to 45° and emits 2–3 shorter, higher calls.

Female may swing head from side to side while calling and walking. Musically, the calls are an antiphonal duet.

To listen to a unison call, go to the website: **www.savingcranes.org/sandhill-crane.html.**

Function: *Affirmation of pair solidarity.* Used to reaffirm territorial claim, for territorial defense, for threat in crowds of cranes, and in aggressive encounters.

Location call

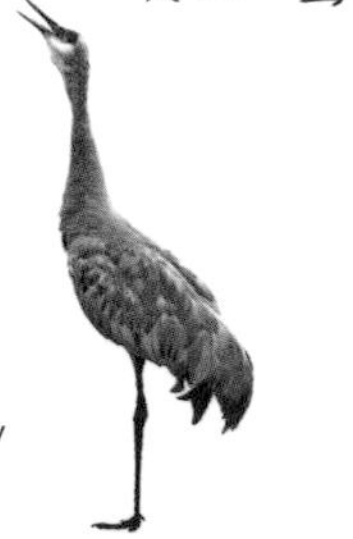

Display: Crane stands with head tilted upward and gives a single loud blast, much like the male segment of the unison call. Location calls may be repeated every 10–15 seconds.

Function: *Maintaining contact with other cranes*, as when members of a pair are foraging separately or when cranes on adjacent territories are monitoring their crane neighbors.

SOCIAL BODY LANGUAGE

Crown contracted

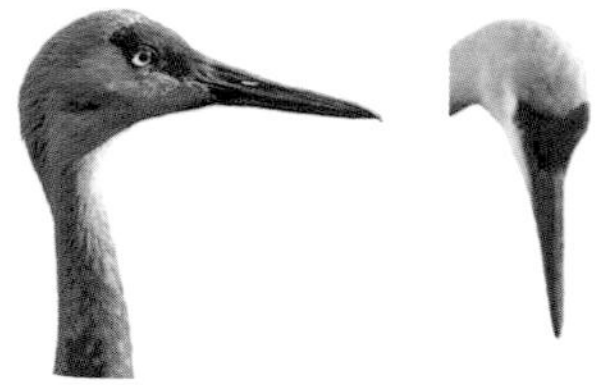

Display: The crown is covered by tiny black narrow feathers that become visible when the crane is relaxed.

The red skin ends just behind the eye.

Function: *Contracted crown indicates that the crane is relaxed and not stressed.*

Crown expanded

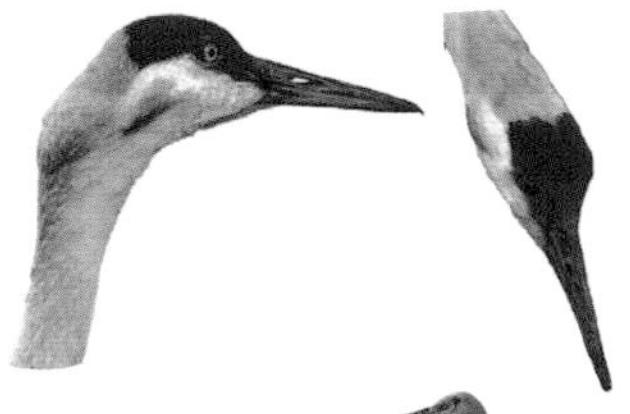

Display: Aroused cranes pull the red patch backward along the top of the head by increasing blood flow and by contracting superficial muscles to flash more red skin.

Function: *Larger (expanded) crown reflects arousal or excitement.* The patch of red skin on the forehead is like a flag.

Tall-investigative

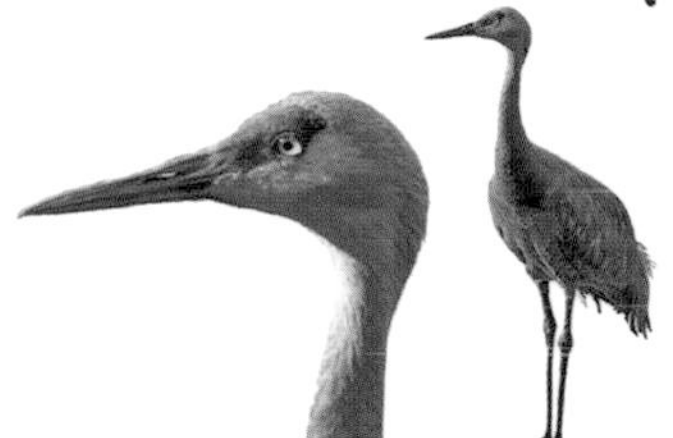

Display: The crane stands still and quietly monitors the surrounding environment with **crown contracted.**

Function: *Signifies cautious vigilance when no threat is visible.* Within a group of foraging cranes, several usually show this display.

Tall-alert

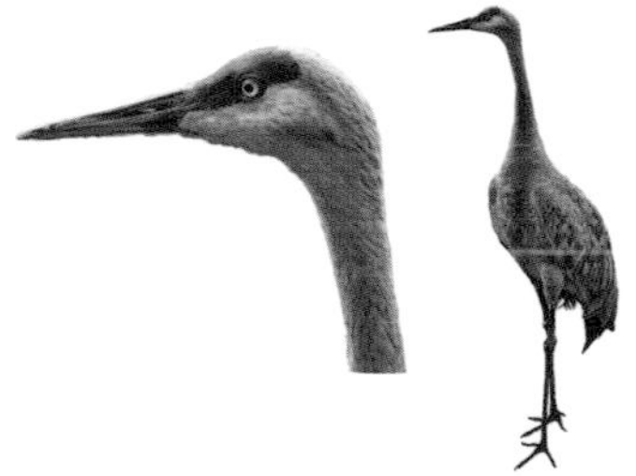

Display: The crane stands tall and still with its head lifted high and **crown expanded**. It stares intently at an intruder.

Function: *Signals that a potential threat is present.* The threat could be a predator or another crane.

Bustle up

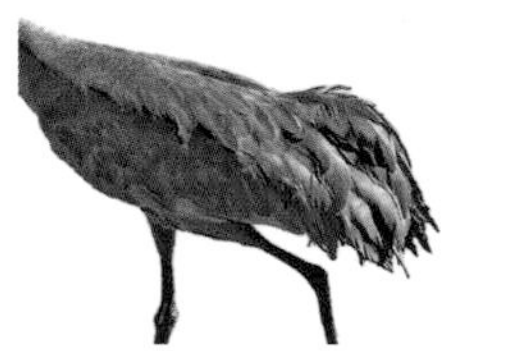

Display: With the wings held close to the body, the innermost flight feathers (called the tertial feathers) attached to the bird's upper wing are raised, giving the impression of a fluffy bustle at the rear.

Function: *Reflects arousal. Bustle-up* is a component of several of the displays below.

Pre-strut & Strut

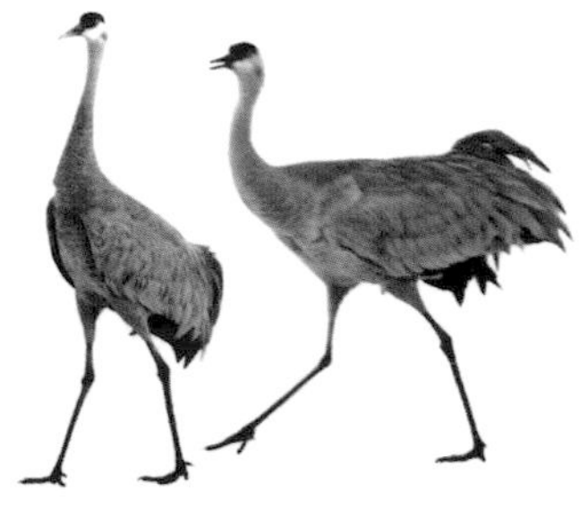

Display: For both **pre-strut** and **strut**, the crane is stiff with feathers sleeked, **crown expanded** and often **bustle up**. In the **pre-strut**, the crane stands still, but in the **strut**, the crane turns sideways to another crane and walks with slow, measured steps, lifting each foot high. The expanded crown may be turned toward the other crane.

Function: *Reflects higher arousal than **tall-alert***. When used as a threat display, it is often followed by a **unison call.**

DANCE

Dancing facilitates pair bonding and allows rivals to assess one another. Pre-adult cranes practice dancing for years before they select a mate. Parents educate their young chicks by dancing with them.

Bow

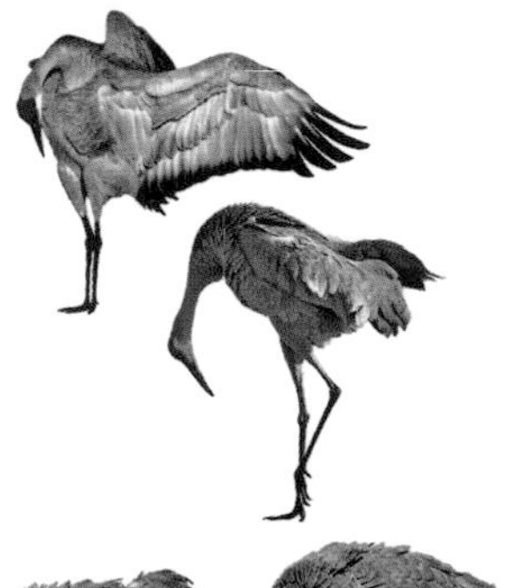

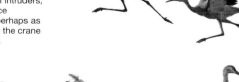

Display: Crane lowers its head, points bill sharply down and arches the neck.

The right image is the typical bow after mating with body almost horizontal and the wings flared slightly out. In the left image, made just after the crane landed, body is vertical and the open wings spread back.

Function: *Ritualized coda after mating. Threat when landing in a crowd of cranes.*

Ruffle-shake, Ruffle-thigh-threat

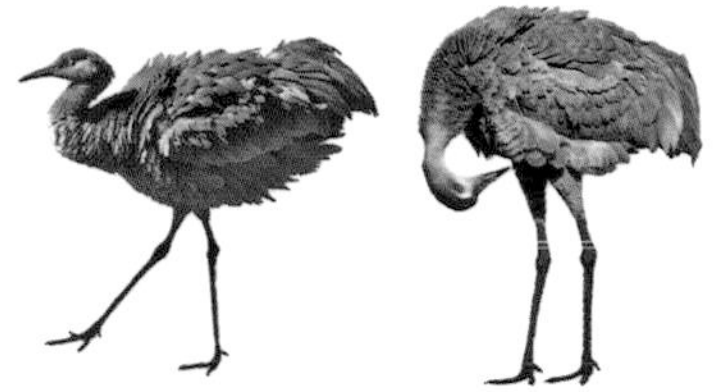

Display: Feathers are fluffed, and neck is pulled back or bowed. Crane may stand still, gyrate, rock from side-to-side or pace forward. Often occurs at the end of a dance.

Function: *Ruffling with expanded crown and simultaneous preening communicates threat.*

Ground-stab

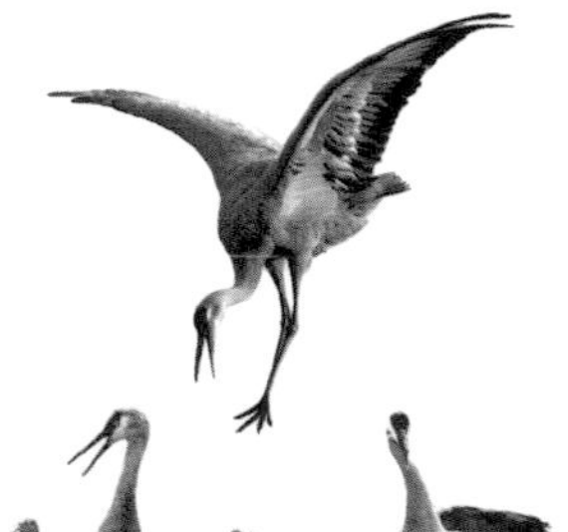

Display: Crane, with wings spread, pecks down at the ground. The next display is often a **wing-spread-hold** or **jump**.

Function: *"Look at me and let's dance!"* In a flock on staging sites, it often recruits a dancing partner to **jump** or **wing-spread-hold.**

Jump

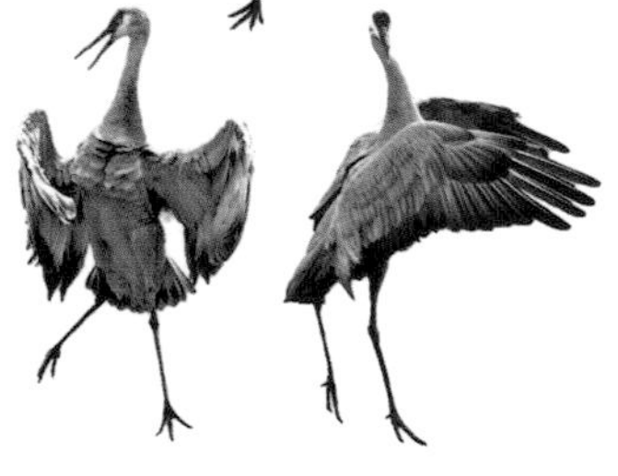

Display: Crane jumps up, often toward a partner or into the wind. Highly variable: wings spread, cupped, or held back, neck upright or pecking down, sometimes vocalizing.

Function: *Dance for courtship or competition, often after **ground-stab**.* May reflect high-spiritedness or even play.

Wing-spread-hold

Display: Crane stands or walks with head pointed forward and with wings held out and often fanned briefly. In left picture below, an adult molting primary feathers is dancing with a 3-week-old chick.

Function: *At the start of dance sequence, often after **ground-stab.***

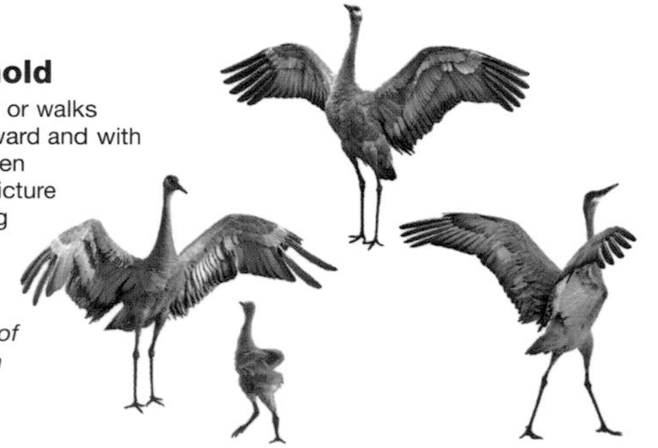

DANCE

Wing-spread-forward-tilt

Display: Body axis tilted forward, neck tightly coiled back, wings spread out with tips curled down.

Function: *Pair and family dance.*

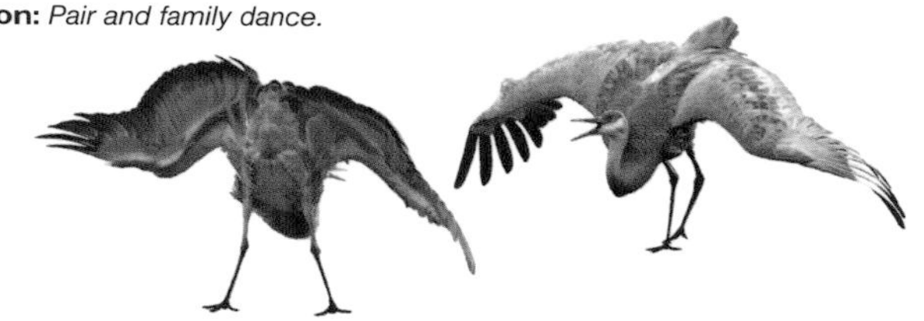

Jump-rake

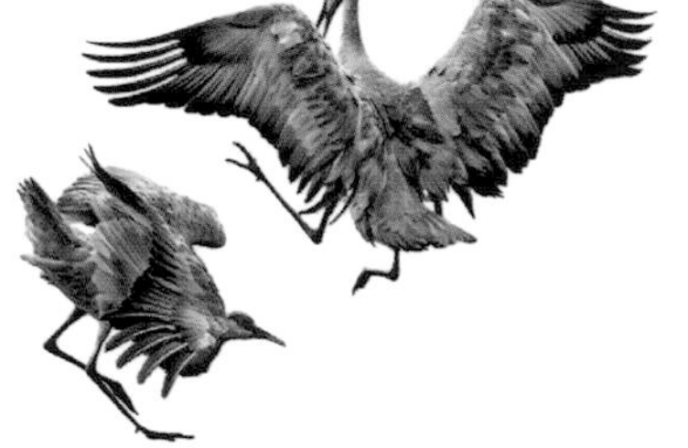

Display: Crane leaps into the air and kicks out toward dance partner. The left bird (female) is in a **wing-spread-forward-tilt**. In dance there is no body contact.

Function: *Dance. Also used in threat and attack* when feet can strike an opponent.

Run-flap

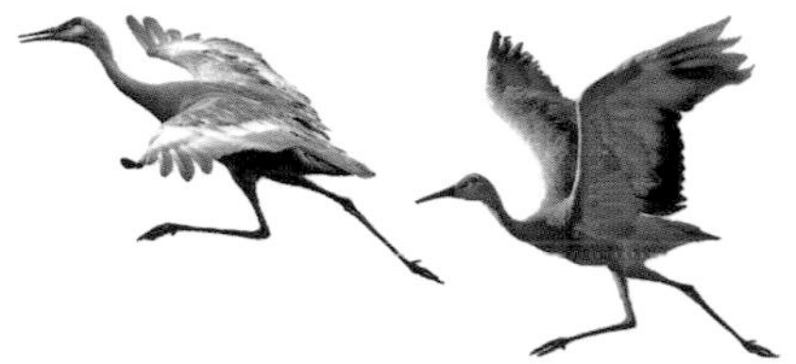

Display: The crane flaps its wings and sprints forward.

Function: *Multipurpose.* Used to gain speed before flight, to threaten intruders, as part of a dance sequence, and perhaps as an expression of the crane equivalent of joy.

Object-toss

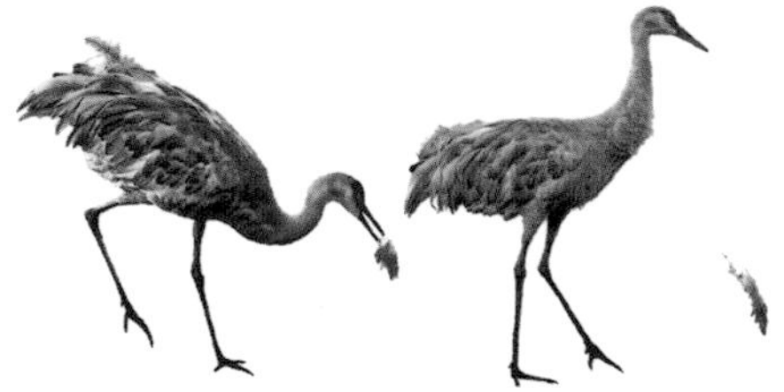

Display: During dancing, crane may seize a feather, twig or grass stem, fling it upward and watch it fall.

Function: *Solo or pair dance.*

Stab-grab-wave

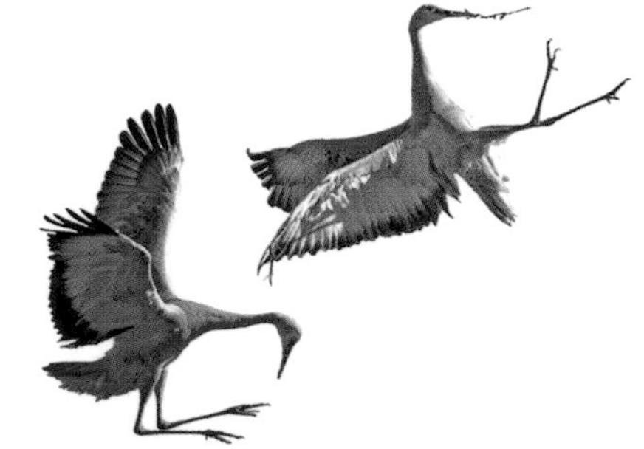

Display: Crane stabs and tugs at a plant on the ground, pulls up vegetation and jumps at an extreme backward angle while waving plant material. In this picture, the male was dancing with a colt.

Function: *Dance.*

Dancing frequently involves circling of one crane around a stationary partner or rotating of both partners. The sequences of linked dance steps below are seen on summer nesting territories but are rare at roosting or staging sites.

Tour-jeté (Jump-turn)
Display: Crane makes three jumps to complete one rotation. The three photos were consecutive, 0.1 seconds apart as crane turned clockwise.
Function: *Often a solo dance, generally by male.*

Minuet
Display: A mated pair with wings extended gracefully rotates. Other displays may be interspersed during the circling.
Function: *Reflects close synchrony of pair.*

Salute
Display: Male crane salutes, standing "at attention" for ~2 seconds while the female runs left-to-right in an arc and then turns toward him to display.
Function: *Pair dance or family dance.*

Run-flap-glide
Display: In the midst of pair dancing, one crane retreats, turns to face its mate, and then rushes forward, first **run-flapping**, next **jumping**, and then **gliding**. The crane lands in front of its mate who responds with a **wing-spread-forward-tilt**. The three photos are a series.
Total elapsed time for the display sequence was 0.2 seconds.
Function: *A rare high-arousal display, usually given by females.*

Single-wing Spin
Display: To facilitate rapid rotation, crane extends its outside (left) wing and pulls the inner one against its body like a spinning figure skater.
- The left bird is a gangly 3-week-old chick dancing with its father.
- The middle bird is a 2-month-old colt.
- The right bird is an adult female dancing with its mate.
Function: *Facilitates rapid circling around a partner.*

Gape & Gape-sweep
Display: Crane spreads wings, partially crouches and holds head forward and down with bill open. Head is swept left and right in **gape-sweep**. The crane in this photo was highly aroused after returning to its nest territory in the spring.
Function: *Response to jump or other steps of dancing partner, or a solo dance.*

Curtsey
Display: Crane squats low with neck coiled back, wings held close to body, and primary feathers spread. This display is one of the first dance displays of young colts. In pair dancing of adults, it is usually given by the female.
Function: *Response to jump or gape of partner.*

Tuck-bob
Display: With neck tightly coiled and bill held horizontal, crane bobs its body up and down. Wings are partially spread, and feathers are sleeked. This dynamic display is often followed by a **jump** or circling.
Function: *Dance.*

Arch
Display: Neck arched up and bill pointed vertically. Wings are lifted and spread. This is a rare display in Sandhill cranes seen after spring return to traditional nesting site.
Function: *Very high arousal ritualized variant of tuck-bob.*

Preening
Display: Cranes devote much time to meticulously combing each flight feather and to rubbing their heads across back and wings.
Function: *Preening keeps feathers aligned and free of contaminants. It ensures that feather barbules can hook together for stability and optimal flight.*

Feather-oiling
Display: Like most birds, cranes have a large preen gland that opens above the base of the tail and produces a mix of oily odorous substances. Head and bill are wiped across the gland opening, and oily secretions are spread over feathers of the wing, back and breast.
Function: *The oils may waterproof the feathers and repel parasites. In other bird species, preen glands emit chemical signals that affect behavior (pheromones).*

Ruffle
Display: Bare skin is contracted and feathers are raised and fluffed all over the body.
Function: *Ruffling is used for grooming to dispel dust and feather dander. Cranes often ruffle after pair dancing.*

Chasing
Display: The crane runs forward with wings flapping and in a stabbing posture. This crane was chasing a duck.
Function: *Dispelling an intruder, especially when young colts are present.*

Cower
Display: The crane lowers its head and retracts its neck. Head feathers are often fluffed. The bird may stand still or walk. This intruder crane was being driven from another's nest territory. In the extreme form, the crane lowers back on its heels to a lying position.
Function: *A very submissive defensive display that is also seen in sick cranes.*

Bill-spar
Display: Two cranes stand tall, face-to-face, **crowns expanded**, vocalizing and pointing their bills toward each other as did these two bachelors.
Function: *Threat and attack that may escalate into jump-rake with feet kicking out at opposing crane.*

Crouch-threat
Display: After standing with **crown expanded**, the crane lowers briefly to the lie position, sleeks its neck feathers, partially spreads and droops its wings, and pecks at vegetation on the ground. Seconds after this display, the female and its mate gave vigorous **unison calls**.
Function: *High-level aggressive threat.*

Horizontal-walk-threat
Display: The displaying crane on the left lowers its head with neck and back held horizontal and walks back and forth repeatedly in front of the intruder who is turning away.
Function: *Threat that encourages intruder to leave.*

Charging-bow
Display: The attacking crane, with head bowed and with wings held up and back, runs toward intruder.
Function: *Threat following horizontal-walk.*

Running-charge-bite
Display: The crane **run-flaps** with bill open, chasing and then biting the intruder who was driven from the territory.
Function: *Attack after charging-bow.*

Bill-down
Display: The crane lowers its head until the bill nearly touches the ground, and the posture is held for several seconds. **Crown is expanded, bustle is up,** and the crane gives a soft purr or growl. This crane was defending its nest territory from a pair of intruding cranes.
Function: *Threat.*

Droop-wing-threat
Display: The crane faces an intruder and droops its wings such that the primary feathers almost touch vegetation. This crane was expelling a fox from the nest territory.
Function: *Threat.*

Wing-leg-stretch
Display: Wing and leg are extended and stretched to the side.
Function: *May be merely flexing muscles.* Three-month old chick at left is stretching before takeoff.

Parade-march
Display: The crane stretches its neck and bill slightly upward and paces slowly with **bustle up** and **crown expanded**.
Function: *Indicates desire for interaction with other cranes, as when the male approaches the female in the mating ritual. This posture might reflect sniffing of sex pheromones.*

Female-receptive
Display: As the female paces forward, turns her back toward the male and spreads her wings, approaches in **parade march** and emits a soft purr.
Function: *The wing-spread posture is her signal to the male that she is ready to mate.*

Treading
Behavior: The male steps upon the back of the female for two to four seconds. After mating, both cranes bow and ruffle.
Function: *Insemination.*

Tenting
Behavior: For the first three to four weeks after hatching, copper-colored crane chicks sleep at night under the protection of their mother's wings. Chicks use the wing-tent to avoid rain, snow or hail and as protection from predation. At bed time, chicks gently peck to ask the female to partially lift her wings.

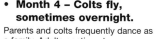

Bathing
Behavior: Cranes bathe by dipping into shallow water and shaking vigorously. Bathing is frequent after a meat meal (vole or duckling) and on dusty staging areas before migration.
Function: *Grooming, cooling on hot days, or dispelling biting insects.* In groups of cranes, the bathing behaviors can be contagious with cranes displaying **(jump, ground-stab** and so forth) as they bathe.

Between two and five years of age, cranes select their mates and then remain paired for decades. Each pair returns to the nest territory that it faithfully occupies from year to year.

- **Month 1 – Cranes build nest, lay eggs and incubate.**

After inspection of the territory upon arrival in late spring, male and female dance.

When a mutually acceptable nest site is selected, both birds gather and pile marsh vegetation. After the female lays two eggs, male and female trade incubation duties for 30 days until hatch.

- **Month 2 – Chicks run, flap their wings and eat.**

Newly hatched chicks sleep under their mother's wings for the first three to four weeks. During the day, they watch their parents closely and try to imitate while running about and waving their tiny wings.

Both adults offer seeds, berries, tubers, insects and meat from voles or ducklings to chicks. The nutrients fuel the transformation of 4-inch downy toddlers into 36-inch colts that are flight-competent for migration.

- **Month 3 – Colts dance and begin preflight training.**

Colts observe adult displays and often face off to dance avidly with a parent. Dancing promotes socialization and provides pre-flight physical conditioning. Parents demonstrate flight to the colts by flying around the nest territory. In addition to being fed by their parents, colts begin to forage on their own.

- **Month 4 – Colts fly, sometimes overnight.**

Parents and colts frequently dance as a family. Adults continue to encourage colts to practice **run-flapping** until they can "catch air," then glide and finally take off in tandem with parents or in solo flights.

Flying and landing skills improve as parents lead colts on hour-long and overnight flight excursions. At summer's end, the family departs the nest territory and joins flocks at a staging area in preparation for southerly migration.

Deeper understanding of crane language might offer insight into the worldview and perhaps even into the mind of a crane. Watch and listen quietly, think about function and share your observations.